FOREWORD

BY DR ROSAMUND CLEAL, CURATOR OF THE ALEXANDER KEI...

Alexander Keiller's life and family history have many features of a historical drama: a feisty female ancestor who dragged her family from obscurity through invention and entrepreneurial skill; brothers divided and a black sheep cast off with barely a penny; disastrous fires and early deaths; Alexander himself orphaned at a young age and devoting himself to a life of riches and pleasure in which sex, speed, women and drink feature in almost equal measure.

But that would be to underplay the complexity of the Keiller family history and to misrepresent Alexander Keiller's life and his contribution to archaeology. Yes, he did spend a great deal of his inheritance on fast cars, skiing, property, and on his four wives and other women, but he spent a great deal more on archaeology. He also spent thousands of pounds on forming important collections of antiquities and books which were given to public institutions. Above all, his work at Avebury transformed a much damaged prehistoric site into one which is now internationally valued as a World Heritage Site. What we know about prehistoric Avebury today is very largely due to Alexander Keiller, and the picturesque and fascinating stone circles that are now enjoyed by many thousands of people appear as they do because of his work.

This guidebook would not have been possible without the work of two authors who have carried out most of the research on the Keiller family: William Mathew (largely on Alexander Keiller's ancestors) and Lynda Murray (author of *A Zest for Life*, the biography of Alexander Keiller), and they are acknowledged with gratitude.

THE KEILLER FAMILY

Alexander Keiller had his great-great-grandmother, Janet Keiller (neé Mathewson), to thank for the family fortune. Janet Mathewson married John Keiller, a Dundee tailor, in 1762. Legend has it that a ship laden with Seville oranges sailed into the port of Dundee, and a member of the Keiller family bought the cargo to give Janet a different fruit to cook with, marmalade being usually made from quinces. In fact, marmalade made from oranges existed before this, both in a firm, sliceable form and as a thinner variety containing pieces of peel. The Keillers appear to have developed the latter and then excelled at marketing it.

Janet and her seventh child, James (born in 1775), appear to have been the leaders in the family business, which began trading sometime around 1800 (1797 is often quoted). The business prospered and factories were eventually opened in Guernsey and London in addition to the Dundee base. By the mid-19th century the firm was managed by Alexander Riddoch Keiller, a grandson of Janet; he married in 1848 and had two sons: James in 1849 and John Mitchell two years later. Both boys joined the family firm but relations between the father and eldest son seem to have been strained. The younger brother, John Mitchell, became a full partner at the age of 21, while the elder was excluded completely from a share in the business when his father died in 1879: the evidence of family letters suggests James's behaviour offended his father and James disappeared from the family history.

In 1884 John Mitchell Keiller married Mary Greig and on 1 December 1889, in Dundee, Mary gave birth to Alexander, the couple's only child. His future in the family business would have seemed assured, but in fact he would take very little part in it and would make his mark in quite a different field: archaeology.

▲ *The marmalade was sold in glass jars and pots like these. By 1867 one and a half million pots alone were needed for the product each year.*

John Mitchell Keiller's health was poor, and, because of this, he retired from the family business in 1893, though he remained as chairman. The Dundee home was sold and the family moved to 13 Hyde Park Gardens, London.

By the time Alexander started at Hazelwood Preparatory School in Limpsfield, Surrey, in the autumn of 1898, his father was spending increasing amounts of time sailing in warmer climes, an antidote to his poor health. But John Keiller's absences meant he was something of a distant father, missing Alexander's homecoming following his first term at school, and the boy and his mother spent Christmas without him.

On 2 January 1899, the day after his 48th birthday, John Mitchell Keiller died at sea, whilst sailing from Madeira to the West Indies. His estate was valued at £435,367, which would be worth around £24 million today, most of which would eventually come to Alexander. Despite two serious factory fires in 1900, one of which entirely destroyed the Dundee factory, by the early years of the 20th century the business Alexander would inherit was in a healthy position, with marmalade immensely popular at the Edwardian breakfast table.

In 1903 Alexander Keiller's education continued at Eton College in Berkshire, although his academic achievements were modest. School holidays saw the boy spending time at Morven, a Scottish estate his father had purchased. It may have been here, in Aberdeenshire, which is rich in stone circles, that his interest in archaeology began.

Keiller's mother died in 1907 and, although still only 17, Alexander left Eton that summer and lived under the guardianship of an uncle.

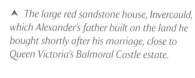

The large red sandstone house, Invercauld, which Alexander's father built on the land he bought shortly after his marriage, close to Queen Victoria's Balmoral Castle estate.

Alexander Keiller aged about 17, at Morven, Aberdeenshire.

COMING OF AGE & INDEPENDENCE

Alexander came into his inheritance when he reached the age of 21 in 1910, and chose to be represented at board meetings by his uncle. Over time he increased his own shareholding and became a little more involved with the business. Occasionally he attended Annual Board Meetings of the company, although, as these were held during the winter, apologies for his absence were often received from St Moritz in Switzerland.

Alexander Keiller's inheritance allowed him to pursue several of his passions, not least skiing, a sport he initially took up at the age of 15. He excelled at cross-country and ski-jumping, and his success led him to take part in the British ski competition in St Moritz in January 1913, where he won the Ski Club of Great Britain cup with a jump of 84 feet 6 inches (25.75 metres).

▲ *Cocktails in the room which now celebrates Alexander Keiller's life in Avebury Manor.*

Skiing remained an interest for most of his life and in 1931 Keiller became president of the Ski Club of Great Britain. As well as the responsibilities of his position he also enjoyed the social life, recording that during an Oxford University Ski Club dinner 'sixteen of us consumed a hundred and fifty cocktails before the meal began. I clearly recall doing my share up to this point, after which I do not very clearly recollect anything.'

◄ *Keiller with an unidentified Scottish standing stone, wearing what is probably the Macgregor tartan, to which he was entitled through his mother's family.*

STONE CIRCLES

An interest undoubtedly sparked by his Scottish background, and perhaps the source of his interest in prehistoric archaeology, was in the stone circles of Aberdeenshire, which he surveyed over several years.

FLORENCE PHIL-MORRIS

On 2 June 1913 Keiller married by Special Licence. Born Florence Marian Morris, the daughter of Philip Richard Morris, an artist of the Royal Academy, his new wife had chosen to embellish her middle name and surname. Her adjustments of the facts did not stop there: although her marriage certificate stated that she was 25 – two years older than her husband – she was actually almost seven years his senior.

THE FIRST WORLD WAR

Keiller's wartime career is not fully known, but on 9 October 1914 he joined the Royal Naval Volunteer Reserve as a Temporary Lieutenant. Within two months he was involved with 'Special Service' for the newly formed Armoured Cars division, a natural fit with his civilian occupation – recorded as 'Motor

▼ *Special Licence for marriage, issued to Alexander Keiller by the Archbishop of Canterbury on 30 May 1913.*

Engineer' – and he served in France from April 1915. Records state that at the end of June 1915 he became Temporary Acting Flight Lieutenant (with Armoured Cars) at Chingford, north-east of London. On 27 November he took his test in an Avro biplane and was awarded his Aviator's Certificate. However, in January the following year he was deemed 'physically unfit', and his commission terminated, although the specific nature of his condition is unknown.

Keiller's wartime career was not yet finished. On 29 July 1918, he was appointed as a Temporary Lieutenant at the Air Ministry; by September he was Staff Officer 3rd class with the Deputy Directorate of Air Intelligence, and subsequently promoted to Temporary Captain. He stayed with Air Intelligence until April 1919, when he was assigned the honorary rank of Captain.

▲ *Alexander and Florence Keiller's marriage certificate, 2 June 1913.*

WESSEX FROM THE AIR

The 1920s saw the most important development of Alexander Keiller's life. In 1920 his life was largely in London and Scotland; by the end of the decade he had formed an association with Wiltshire which would last beyond his death. Key to this change was a solitary and eccentric man who would also have an impact on 20th-century archaeological practice: Osbert Guy Stanhope Crawford (1886–1957).

O.G.S. Crawford, as he was usually known, was the first Archaeological Officer at the Ordnance Survey and had a keen interest in aerial surveying. In the summer of 1923 he wrote a series of articles in the *Observer* about this new technique. On 29 July 1923 Alexander Keiller wrote to Crawford, citing the *Observer* articles and explaining that he had long been interested in the idea and would be willing to fund some work: 'I cannot but think,' he wrote, 'that such an aerial survey might provide really invaluable results.'

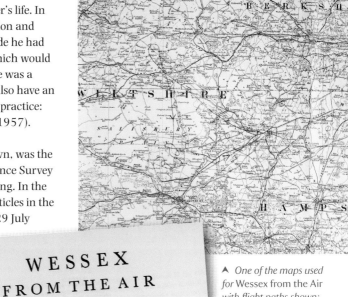

▲ *One of the maps used for* Wessex from the Air *with flight paths shown; now in the Alexander Keiller Museum, Avebury.*

WESSEX FROM THE AIR

By
O. G. S. CRAWFORD, F.S.A.
and
ALEXANDER KEILLER
F.S.A., F.G.S.

with contributions by
R. C. C. CLAY, M.R.C.S., L.R.C.P., F.S.A.
ERIC GARDNER, M.B., F.S.A.

◀ *Title page of* Wessex from the Air.

Below left: O.G.S. Crawford (partially hidden) at Windmill Hill.

As a result, in early summer 1924, from a base at Weyhill Aerodrome, near Andover in Hampshire, Crawford and Keiller flew in a de Havilland, taking photographs which would record traces of archaeological sites on the ground. (Years later Keiller travelled to America in the *Hindenburg* airship and – perhaps recalling the difficulties of using the de Havilland – jokingly told a young friend that it would be the perfect vehicle for archaeological aerial photography as it moved slowly and even had a bar.)

From 300 photographs, 50 were selected and plans were produced showing the archaeological features present in each. *Wessex from the Air*, by Crawford and Keiller, was published in 1928. Alexander Keiller had been quite correct in his prediction: the results were 'really invaluable' and have stood the test of time. Crawford and Keiller's work was not the earliest aerial photography for archaeological purposes, but it was the first major publication on the subject.

A NEW VENTURE

lthough Alexander Keiller is best known for his work on the stone settings at Avebury, his reputation as an archaeologist does not rest on that work alone. His first excavation in England was of a Neolithic site on Windmill Hill, about one mile north-west of Avebury. This was the first large-scale excavation of such a site in the country.

ACQUIRING WINDMILL HILL

In August 1923, O.G.S. Crawford circulated a letter explaining that there were plans for a private wireless station and housing at Avebury and that this would ruin the setting of the monuments. Fortunately government approval for the scheme was soon refused, not because of the archaeology but because of the danger to local planes from the high masts. Keiller wrote jokingly to Crawford in the September: 'I should have preferred that the

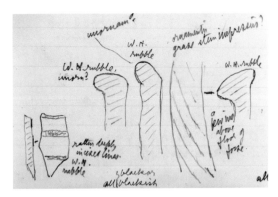

▲ Sketches of Neolithic pottery from Windmill Hill in the Reverend H.G.O. Kendall's notebook.

archaeologists of Britain should have defended the site by force, armed with weapons of the period', but Crawford continued to be worried about the site.

In the spring of 1924 Crawford was involved with local clergyman the Reverend H.G.O. Kendall in discussing the possible purchase of the site with the landowner. Crawford seems to have suggested to Kendall that he had a likely purchaser but it was only late in the proceedings that he wrote to Keiller suggesting he might buy the site. 'The Windmill Hill proposition is startling,' Keiller wrote. But by June he had bought the land and his important association with Avebury had begun.

The Entrance of Kennet avenue into Abury 14 May 1724.

◄ Windmill Hill is seen in the distance in this view of Avebury by William Stukeley, published in 1743.

EARLY INFLUENCES

In the 1740s the antiquary William Stukeley published his research on the Avebury area. He recorded that 'there is a very delicate hill north of Abury, of a round form, with an easy ascent quite round; 'tis called "Windmill-hill". The turf as soft as velvet. 'Tis encompass'd with a circular trench, exceeding old.'

Early in the 20th century, H.G.O. Kendall, rector of a neighbouring parish, collected hundreds of worked flints from the surface of Windmill Hill and in 1922–23 investigated a ditch there which produced Neolithic pottery. Two more circuits of ditches, surviving as shallow depressions in the ground, were later recognised and we now know that the three concentric ditches on the hill were dug around 5,600 years ago.

EXCAVATIONS AT WINDMILL HILL 1925-29

The Neolithic site at Windmill Hill is what is known as a 'causewayed enclosure'. These are sites dating to the earlier part of the Neolithic period (New Stone Age); most of them were built around 5,600 years ago. They were probably not permanent settlements, but were occupied for parts of the year.

Alexander Keiller conducted five seasons of excavation on Windmill Hill, from 1925 to 1929. Although other causewayed enclosures were excavated during the 1920s it was Windmill Hill that had the most impact. Until late in the 20th century the earlier Neolithic period in southern Britain was known as the Windmill Hill Culture. This was partly due to the scale of the excavations and the vast quantities of stone tools, pottery and animal bones which were excavated, and from which it was possible for archaeologists to form an idea of Neolithic life.

Causewayed enclosures like Windmill Hill usually have more than one circuit of ditch, broken by many small 'causeways' of undug bedrock; only some of these are proper entrances, the others seeming to mark breaks between the groups who originally dug the ditch and perhaps also having some symbolic purpose.

WOMEN OF WINDMILL HILL

By the end of the excavations, three of the four members of the supervisory staff were women: Veronica Keiller (the second Mrs Keiller) took a leading role, as did her sister, Dorothy Liddell, who went on to direct other excavations herself. Kay Duncan, the youngest of the three, was an important site assistant and became very close to Alexander Keiller. Later on

VERONICA LIDDELL

The year 1924 was notable for Keiller not only because of his purchase of Windmill Hill, but also for his marriage, on 29 February, to Veronica Liddell. Veronica was the sister of a famous First World War pilot, Aiden Liddell, who had been acclaimed as a national hero in 1915 when he was awarded the Victoria Cross and later died of his wounds. Nothing is known of how she and Alexander met, but she was certainly interested in archaeology. When Keiller wrote to O.G.S. Crawford about the possible purchase of Windmill Hill, he said: 'I showed your letter to my wife, who was very keen on the thought until she discovered that there was a possibility of excavating dwellings there, whereupon she went completely mad ...'

The newlyweds took up residence in Charles Street, in what had been Keiller's occasional London home. Soon after, Keiller purchased the adjoining property and converted the two houses into one, which came to house his museum, map room, study and drawing office.

➤ *Veronica, the second Mrs Keiller, during the excavations at Windmill Hill.*

Keiller wrote that he had intended the first Curator of his museum to be another of his assistants, Marjorie James, but she left when she married, before her appointment. This preponderance of women in such roles was unusual for the time and shows a confidence on Keiller's part that women were capable as archaeologists, particularly as he expected all his staff to work to very high standards.

▲ Excavating and recording one of the ditches at Windmill Hill.

SKELETONS

One of the features of Windmill Hill was that several almost complete skeletons of animals were found in the ditches, including this dog now on display in the Alexander Keiller Museum at Avebury; it would have been similar to a modern fox terrier. Keiller liked to assign nicknames and the skeleton was known as 'Felstead' after the winner of the Derby at the time it was found.

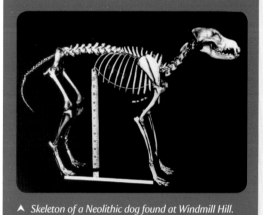

▲ Skeleton of a Neolithic dog found at Windmill Hill.

▲ The Windmill Hill excavation team in 1928. Back row from left to right (surnames only recorded): Dobson, Rogers, White, Rogers, Pearce, Goddard, Pratt; front row: supervisory staff and Keiller: W.E.V. (William) Young, Veronica Keiller, Alexander Keiller, Dorothy Liddell, Kay Duncan.

MOTOR CARS & OTHER INTERESTS

▼ *Alexander Keiller's own Sizaire-Berwick which was purchased by the National Trust in 1996 and is now displayed in the Museum at Avebury.*

At the time of his marriage to Florence, before the First World War, Keiller recorded his profession as 'Motor Agent'. Just two weeks after his wedding he was registered as a Director and main investor of Sizaire-Berwick (France) Limited – a company formed from the coming together of French-based Sizaire-Naudin and London-based F.W. Berwick and Co. Ltd.

Sizaire-Berwick's London office was in Berkeley Street and the factory was situated close to Paris. The 20hp 4-cylinder Sizaire-Berwick was first shown in Paris in October 1913, and was well received. Until the outbreak of the First World War, when the factory was taken over for wartime production, the cars were built at the rate of five per week. Before the war the company employed the future 'Dixon

WILLIAM STUKELEY (1687-1765)

William Stukeley was an antiquary who published a major work on Avebury (*Abury*) in 1743, 20 years after he had spent five summers studying the monuments there, from 1719-24, at a time when many of the stones were being broken up for building purposes.

In the early 1920s Alexander Keiller bought many of Stukeley's manuscripts and notes. This eventually drew his interest to the Avebury stone circles and in the 1930s he also encouraged one of his assistants, Stuart Piggott, to investigate Stukeley's life, Piggott becoming his first biographer. In the 1950s Keiller gave his Stukeley collection to the Bodleian Library, Oxford.

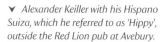

> ➤ The Citroën Kegresse during the Windmill Hill excavations, with Keiller standing, left, and the female members of the Windmill Hill staff.

➤ Alexander Keiller with his Hispano Suiza, which he referred to as 'Hippy', outside the Red Lion pub at Avebury.

of Dock Green', Jack Warner, as a driver, and after the war one of the most famous women of the First World War, nurse Mairi Chisholm, delivered cars to clients. Miss Chisholm, who had been briefly almost as celebrated as Florence Nightingale, was also for a time Keiller's chauffeuse. After the war the company was less successful and the British part ceased trading in 1924.

Alexander Keiller's passion for fast cars did not end with the Sizaire-Berwick and throughout at least the 1920s and 1930s he was buying motor cars. On one occasion, driving through France in the mid-1920s, he was – unusually for him – overtaken by another car. He later saw the vehicle – an Hispano-Suiza – parked outside a hotel and, after negotiating with its owner, Keiller bought it. Known as the 'Tulipwood Car', it was generally acknowledged as astonishingly beautiful. Keiller's collection also included Bugatti racing cars and at least one MG Midget about which he enthused that he could never wish for a better car.

Keiller's cars created much interest during visits to Scotland, when people would come out of their homes to see him roar past and he loved to drive at speed. But his collection also included at least one more practical vehicle: in 1923 Keiller told O.G.S. Crawford that he had just purchased a Citroën Kegresse half track motor. These were early 'off-road' vehicles which could cross difficult terrain easily. Keiller's Citroën Kegresse, which he called 'The Oobit', came into its own at Windmill Hill, where it took the banks and ditches in its stride.

Keiller's interest in motor cars nearly killed him. On 9 July 1929 Keiller and Kay Duncan were involved in what was, Keiller wrote later, 'certainly the worst crash in a car that I am ever likely to have, short of actually being killed'. They had been climbing the hill east of Marlborough 'at a reasonable speed, but not by any manner of means, I consider, an excessive one, viz. some 84 miles per hour, when my back axle broke, and, the car turning round and rising into the air, we hurtled ourselves on to the angular portion of the Bridge'. Both of them broke shoulder blades and Keiller also sustained serious internal injuries.

WITCHCRAFT

Throughout his life Alexander Keiller had a keen interest in the occult, particularly 16th-century witchcraft in Scotland. By the time of his death his library included a large section dedicated to 'Witchcraft, Demonology and Devil-lore', with over 400 volumes dating back to 1489; they were eventually given to the National Library in Edinburgh. Keiller also wrote on the subject, one article being published in the journal *Folklore* in 1922.

CHANGING DIRECTION

After the end of the 1929 Windmill Hill season Keiller conducted no excavations in the Avebury area until 1934. At the same time his private life was also changing and his plans for Avebury developed.

KAY DUNCAN

Kay Duncan (born 1905) became part of what Keiller termed the permanent Windmill Hill staff sometime between 1925 and 1929. During 1929 references appear to Miss Duncan in Keiller's letters, and she visited Morven with him on more than one occasion, in 1930 Keiller recording that they had a wonderful two-day run up to Morven in his new MG motor car.

Eventually Keiller asked Veronica for a divorce and Kay to marry him, but she refused, probably because to marry a divorced man would have been too upsetting for her family. She left Keiller's employment in 1932 and married in 1935. She died in 1986 in Mallorca.

STUART PIGGOTT

In 1933, Alexander Keiller asked a 23-year-old archaeologist, Stuart Piggott, to come and work for him, having recognised the promise the young man showed. Piggott was interested in William Stukeley

▲ *Kay Duncan and Alexander Keiller at Windmill Hill.*

and in his description of the West Kennet Avenue, and Keiller and Piggott drove to Avebury in the Hispano-Suiza to view the surviving standing and fallen stones. It was enough to start Keiller off on his new project, and two seasons of work followed, in 1934 and 1935.

WEST KENNET AVENUE

When first built, over 4,000 years ago, West Kennet Avenue consisted of around 100 pairs of standing stones, running in a sinuous path from the southern entrance of the stone circle at Avebury to a smaller stone circle on Overton Hill. A great number of the stones in the Avenue were broken up in the

◀ *Stuart Piggott and Alexander Keiller in the garden at Avebury Manor, mid-1930s.*

▲ *Raising one of the stones on West Kennet Avenue.*

▶ *Alexander Keiller during the West Kennet Avenue excavations. He is in very few photographs from the Avebury excavations as he took most of them himself.*

ANOTHER DIVORCE

In 1933, Veronica finally left Charles Street and moved back to her family home in Hampshire. Her leaving appears to have upset Keiller, who locked himself in his room for several days, bulletins being issued to Piggott by Frazer, Keiller's Jeeves-like butler. Despite this reaction, and following several attempts on Veronica's part at reconciliation, they were divorced in November 1934. Veronica remarried three years later, and died in 1964.

18th century and others had been buried from the later Middle Ages for unknown reasons. By the time Keiller's work began nine fallen stones were visible in the northernmost third of the Avenue, and just four standing, one of which had been re-erected earlier in the century.

Keiller's excavation of the site took place during 1934 and 1935, assisted by many of the original Windmill Hill team. An important part of the plan from the beginning was to restore the monument to its original condition, so stones which were fallen and those found buried were to be re-erected.

In the case of the first stone to be raised, 12 men took only four days to achieve it without modern equipment, except for steel ropes. Keiller was surprised, expecting it to have taken much longer.

As each stone was re-erected it was made secure with concrete, hidden by its grassy surround. Keiller told a friend that he thought the noise from the cement mixers was a beautiful sound, as it meant the stones would now be standing 3000 years after he'd gone. The same friend noticed that when he referred to a stone he called it 'she'.

Over the course of the two seasons, the original positions of 63 stones were located; 27 of these remained, including 23 fallen stones which were re-erected. Those missing were marked by stelae (upright slabs of concrete) which Keiller designed himself, thus indicating how the original section of the Avenue would have looked. Four graves and an earlier occupation site were also identified, making it one of the most interesting Neolithic sites being excavated at that time.

▶ *A view of the Avenue, looking south, in 1908.*

AVEBURY HENGE

Alexander Keiller had a long-term plan for 14 years' work at Avebury, to include not only two years' work on the West Kennet Avenue but also several seasons on the henge and stone circles. He also wanted to investigate whether another stone avenue existed to the west, as William Stukeley had thought in the 18th century. Keiller considered the state of the henge to be a disgrace, calling it 'this archaeological disgrace of Great Britain' and the condition of the stones 'pathetic and regrettable'. He was particularly concerned about the north-west sector, where trees had been planted over the bank and ditch, and it was there he began his work, in 1937.

After 1937 Keiller conducted two more seasons of excavation: in 1938 on the south-west sector and in 1939 on the south-east. The 1937 and 1938 excavations were intended to locate buried stones and stone-holes of the Outer Circle, but the last was an area excavation of a large part of the interior of one of the inner circles. This type of large area excavation was quite advanced for its time.

HENGES

Henges (usually around 4,500 years old) are areas of land encircled by a bank and ditch, the ditch lying inside the bank. Because this arrangement is impractical for defence, and because henges often show no sign that they have been occupied, they are thought likely to have been intended for religious purposes. Many had elaborate arrangements of wooden or stone uprights inside them. At Avebury there were once three circles of standing stones: one of about 100 stones running just inside the line of the ditch and two smaller circles inside.

▼ *The north-west sector today showing the stones of the Outer Circle encircled by the ditch; most of them had been buried or built into a wall and were re-erected by Keiller. The building in the distance lies on the line of the bank, here destroyed in the late 1600s.*

AN ADDITION TO THE KEILLER CIRCLE: DORIS CHAPMAN

Keiller's first contact with Doris Chapman is not recorded, but by late 1935 at least one writer was referring to her as his mistress. Doris was an artist and worked with Keiller on visual reconstructions of faces from Neolithic skulls. He described her in a letter as 'one of the best, as well as one of the most intelligent, not to say intellectual, assistants I have ever had'. The relationship was clearly a close one and in November 1938 she became the third Mrs Keiller.

▲ *Doris Keiller in a greenhouse at Avebury Manor.*

◄ *Tree roots on the north-west bank were removed by explosives and one explosion sent a piece of timber flying on to Piggott's head, to the amusement of Keiller. He later wrote to another member of the team: 'It is well, I think, for these youngsters to experience some of the horrors which we veterans underwent, with relative cheerfulness, in the Ypres salient in 1915.'*

➤ *The south-west sector under excavation in 1938.*

THE BARBER SURGEON STONE

This stone, here being re-erected in 1938, was found in the south-west sector. Next to it in the burial pit was the skeleton of a man, probably killed when the stone slipped prematurely when it was being buried. Because he was found with tools and scissors it is thought he may have been a 'barber surgeon', as some of Keiller's ancestors were.

➤ *W.E.V. Young by the 'Barber Surgeon Stone'.*

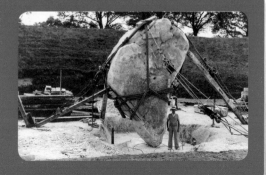

AVEBURY MANOR

While staying at the Red Lion pub during the West Kennet Avenue excavation in the early 1930s, Keiller woke his new assistant Stuart Piggott in the night to tell him his latest idea. He intended, he explained, to buy Avebury Manor and move his collections from Charles Street to Avebury. He was as good as his word, renting the Manor from 1935 and buying it in January 1937. It then became the centre for what Keiller termed the Morven Institute of Archaeological Research.

Keiller confessed in a letter that his 'personal sanctum' – his bedroom and dressing room – possessed 'that indescribable degree of personal discomfort which can only come from exclusively period furniture of the middle of the 16th century'. The rest of the Manor was furnished with many antiques, including several four-poster beds. A Mrs Lillie, Keiller's secretary in 1937, recalled 60 years later that many of the letters she typed had been about buying antiques.

In 1938 a newcomer joined Keiller's archaeological staff: Denis Grant King, an artist. In a diary of his time at Avebury he gives us a glimpse of a lunch party in the Manor, in what is now the Keiller Parlour; it consisted of 'various meats arranged at a side table, where Head, the young under-butler, carved, and from which he brought potato, ground very fine, salad and everything required in a most embarrassingly attentive manner. Before taking our seats, however, we started with wines and cocktails, A.K. pouring out and handing the flask to Cook [the museum curator] for shaking. I am really uncertain what I drank, and avoided expressing likes and dislikes through fear of exposing my abysmal ignorance.'

▲ Keiller's Dressing Room and 'personal sanctum' in the East wing of the Manor.

◄ The oldest part of Avebury Manor appears to have been built in the mid-16th century but was enlarged about 50 years later, around 1600.

THE MUSEUM

By the spring of 1938, Keiller had moved his private museum collection from London to the converted stables in the grounds of Avebury Manor. The new museum was opened on 1 June by Thomas Kendrick, Keeper of the Department of British and Medieval Antiquities at the British Museum, and its opening reported in *The Times* newspaper.

Among the many exhibits from Windmill Hill and West Kennet Avenue, Stuart Piggott had included a broken Keiller's marmalade jar found on West Kennet Avenue: Keiller, fortunately for Piggott, found it very funny. The museum was an immediate success, welcoming 6,429 visitors in the first five months.

▲ This picture, taken in the 1950s, shows the original layout of the Museum. Particularly idiosyncratic are the skulls of cattle from Windmill Hill, displayed as if they were hunting trophies.

COW-CREAMER COLLECTION

As well as Neolithic artefacts, Keiller formed other large collections, including 667 ceramic cow-creamers; for these Keiller kept a 'Herd Book' in which each one was recorded individually and named. An Avebury resident recalled him begging her mother to sell him a cream jug sitting on her dresser; she rejected the generous sum he offered for the piece. On his death, the collection was donated to what is now The Potteries Museum and Art Gallery in Stoke-on-Trent.

▲ One of the Keiller collection of cow creamers, containers for serving milk or cream. They were popular from the 18th century and are still produced today.

▲ One of the 1938 displays from the Museum, featuring the objects found with the 'barber surgeon' and a model demonstrating how the stones were originally erected.

The displays were not only of prehistoric finds: Keiller was careful to keep and record artefacts from later periods – something not all archaeologists of the time did when excavating prehistoric sites. He also held modern views about the value of a museum, writing once: 'Far more use should be made of reconstructions and models ... than is present customary in museums, the function of which is not only to teach the public, but to persuade them to want to learn.'

AN ENDING – AND A BEGINNING

By the end of 1938 a significant dent had been made in Keiller's fortune. This was not the first time he had complained of hardship, although it was probably the most serious. In 1935 he had told the novelist Antonia White that he had suffered a 'monstrous crash' and that his mistress (later the third Mrs Keiller) picked up very effective brooches at Woolworths and could not have new evening frocks.

THE SECOND WORLD WAR

By the summer of 1939 the threat of war was an ever-present cloud and on 3 September the site diary read simply: 'War declared on Germany.' Although work continued until 21 December, this year saw the end of the Avebury excavations.

Keiller was 50 at the beginning of December 1939 and he did not rejoin the services: his war service took the form of working for the Special Constabulary. Ever conscientious, he studied for police exams and became a fingerprint expert.

▲ *Alexander Keiller in his police uniform; he held the rank of Inspector.*

MARITAL PROBLEMS

During the first three years of the war, Doris Keiller worked as a nurse in London. Both she and Keiller had affairs, but although there was a reconciliation, eventually they lived separately. After the war Keiller became involved with Gabrielle Style, a highly successful amateur golfer. When they met in 1947 he was 57 and Gabrielle nearly 20 years his junior. Gabrielle, like Keiller, had been married twice before and it was not until 1951 that they were able to marry, within days of Keiller's divorce from Doris. (Doris remarried two weeks later.) In the same year Keiller had an operation on his throat and four years later, on 29 October 1955, he died of cancer. Gabrielle never remarried and died in 1995. Both her ashes and Keiller's are buried on a small plot of land Keiller retained at Morven.

◀ *Gabrielle Keiller at Windmill Hill in the 1950s during an excavation she commissioned after her husband's death.*

SALES AND GIFTS

In 1943 Keiller sold his land at Avebury to the National Trust, which then placed it in Guardianship with the nation. He retained the Manor and the museum collections, but in 1955, in the spring before he died, he sold the Manor to botanist Sir Francis Knowles.

ALEXANDER KEILLER: HIS WORK

Alexander Keiller's own evaluation of his standing as an archaeologist was surprisingly modest and clear-sighted. He wrote on one occasion that 'I am an archaeological surveyor and excavator when all is said and done' rather than a thinker about archaeological theories. Modern opinion would probably concur with Keiller's own evaluation of himself as an archaeologist, but it can also be recognised today that his work in presenting archaeology to the public was astonishingly bold and ahead of its time.

During Alexander Keiller's lifetime he wrote only rarely about his motivation for the work he did, but occasionally he was more forthcoming. In early 1937 Keiller wrote several letters about the work he intended to carry out at Avebury, explaining that he wanted to 'improve and preserve this great monument of ours ... and render it both accessible to the archaeological student and to members of the interested public'. He also described his work on Windmill Hill since the end of his excavations there: he had had the area fenced, but had also provided gates for 'the convenience of the visiting public' and explanatory descriptions and plans 'to render the site as intelligible to visitors as possible'. Later he even re-emptied the ditches he had excavated and lined them with turf so that visitors could appreciate them.

In Avebury village his work was more controversial. Keiller is often cited as the person who removed many houses from the village in an attempt to restore the henge to its Neolithic condition. Although he supported the idea, he actually removed only three houses and some other structures. Many more were removed later, years after he had sold his land in the village. He also commented on the difficulties for young people in the village to find somewhere to live and wrote that he only supported the removal of houses which had already been condemned as unfit for habitation by the local authorities, as was common at that time.

> 'I am carrying out my work (or endeavouring to do so) in order that those who are not professional archaeologists may the better have, as time proceeds, a sounder basis upon which scientifically to build up an ever increasing knowledge of the prehistoric cultures of this country.'

➤ *Demolition taking place during the excavations of 1938.*

ALEXANDER KEILLER: THE MAN

Alexander Keiller's character remains elusive. On the one hand he could be seen as the typical playboy: thrill-seeking on the ski-jumps and slopes, driving cars recklessly fast, and treating his multiple wives and lovers in a cavalier fashion. On the other, he gave women responsibility on his excavations and in his museum at a time when archaeology was still largely a man's world. Above all, he carried out his archaeological work with a huge commitment of time, energy and money. It is quite clear that archaeology was really his ruling passion. The part of the traditional 'playboy' does not, when his life is examined in detail, fit him very well.

Thanks to Keiller's passion, the monuments at Avebury remain cared for and open to the public. His work at Avebury and Windmill Hill was published in 1965 by Dr Isobel Smith, commissioned by Gabrielle Keiller. In the following year Gabrielle gifted the museum collection to the nation. The museum, which had been known as 'Avebury Museum' in Keiller's lifetime, was re-named the Alexander Keiller Museum.

It remains, perhaps, to give the last words on this complicated and contradictory man to some of the people who knew him:

Denis Grant King (site assistant 1938–39): 'He is a tall, well-built man, with brown hair, a good-shaped head ... and an interesting somewhat furrowed face. He looks distinguished and speaks with distinction. His conversation like his letter-writing is voluminous.'

Miss Elisabeth Neal (temporary secretary 1937): 'He did have a wonderful sense of humour; a very good employer, very generous, and kind.'

Stuart Piggott (chief site assistant and later Professor of Archaeology at Edinburgh University), speaking (in 1995) on why Keiller was sometimes unpopular in the profession: '... because he didn't care a damn for anybody and was prepared to say so and had money to carry it [the work he wanted to do] out.'

From Alexander Keiller's obituary in the British Ski Year Book of 1956: 'Working with him, of course, was never hard work. His inexhaustible, almost boyish enthusiasm and quite unique personal charm carried everyone along and made everything fun.'

➤ Keiller's attention to detail, particularly for archaeological plans and surveys, was well known.

Back cover: Alexander Keiller in the late 1920s.

Used with the kind permission of the family of P.C. Duncan.